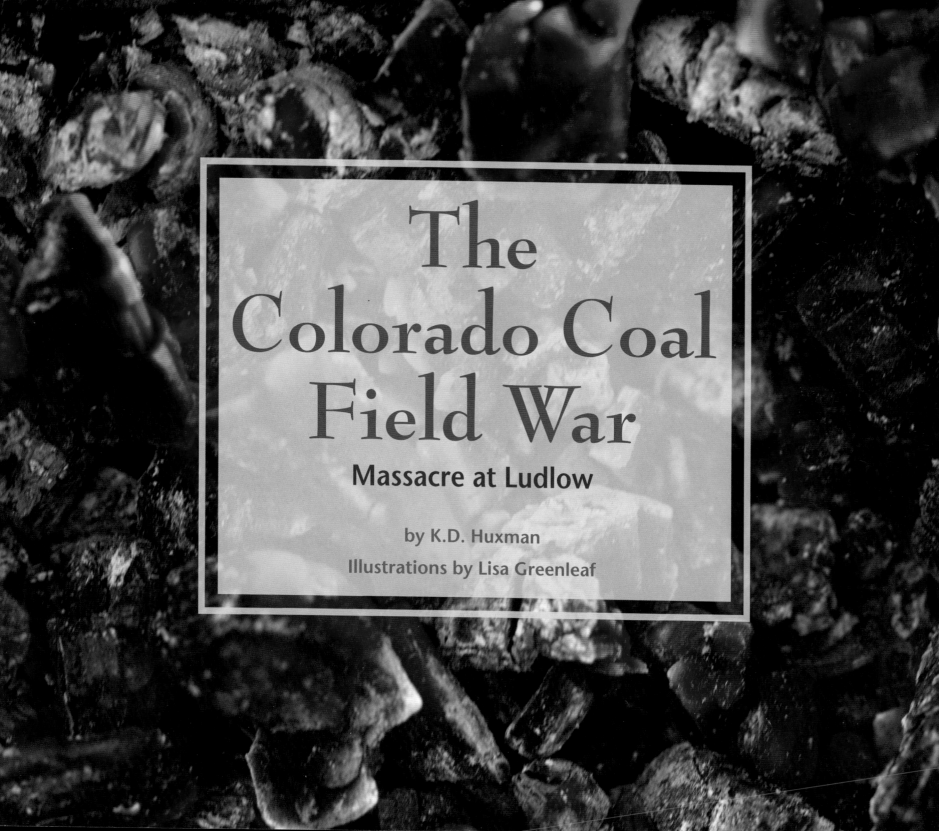

The Colorado Coal Field War

Massacre at Ludlow

by K.D. Huxman

Illustrations by Lisa Greenleaf

Dedication

Many thanks to Mur for opening this door. Much love and thanks to Jay for everything else. ~K.D. Huxman

To Sheila, one of the strongest, kindest, and loving friends I know. I'm thrilled your talents continue to shine throughout the ASB products. ♥ Lisa Greenleaf

Apprentice Shop Books, LLC
Amherst, New Hampshire

Text copyright ©2018

For information regarding permissions contact:
　Apprentice Shop Books, LLC
　Box 375
　Amherst, NH 03031
　www.apprenticeshopbooks.com

LIBRARY OF CONGRESS CATALOGING-IN-PUBLICATION DATA

Huxman, K.D.
　Colorado Cold Field War: Massacre at Ludlow; Illustrations by Lisa Greenleaf
　p.cm. – Once, in America Series
　Includes glossary and index
　1. Colorado Coal Field War—History—the 1900s—juvenile literature

ISBN-13:978-0-9850144-2-1

Printed in United States of America

Cover design, illustrations, and book design by Lisa Greenleaf
Greenleaf Design Studio www.Lisagreenleaf.com

Table of Contents:

Once, in America. . .

. . . coal was king.

But, if you were an immigrant miner who just wanted to be paid an honest day's pay for an honest day's work, you might end up dead.

Your family, too.

It happened in 1914 in a place near the tiny railroad town of Ludlow, Colorado.

Chapter 1:
Louis Tikas and the Immigrant Miners

Louis Tikas

Hoping for Streets of Gold

Louis Tikas was a soft spoken man who grew up in a village near Rethymon, Crete, Greece. He left for the United States in 1906.

Louis turned twenty on his voyage across the Atlantic Ocean. He'd been led to believe America's streets were paved with gold. Opportunities existed for young men willing to work hard. He had lots of company. Between 1901 and 1910 about 170,000 Greeks entered the United States. They left the Old Country for the new in search of jobs that were unavailable at home. The market for currants, a major crop in Greece, had fallen. Immigrants swarmed America's shores not only from Greece, but also from Italy, Austria,

Serbia, Croatia, Germany, Romania, and Japan to name only a few. These were mostly uneducated young men who often could not read or write in their own language let alone understand English.

The first stop for many immigrants from Europe arriving in America was Ellis Island in New York. After they passed a physical and were allowed into the country they **dispersed**. Either they found friends or family who came ahead of them or, like Louis Tikas, they found the employment agent who had convinced them to make the long journey. The agent took them to their new jobs.

Island of Hope, Island of Tears – Ellis Island

In the early twentieth century, one of the first sights an immigrant would see as their ship came into New York harbor was the Statue of Liberty. Their first stop was Ellis Island, the processing center for immigrants. If the person had traveled **steerage**, he had to pass a medical examination to make sure he was not carrying **infectious diseases** into the country. If he failed the examination he could be sent back to his country of origin. If severely ill, he would stay in the Ellis Island Hospital until either getting better, or dying. If he was healthy, he could go on to New York City and the future.

A passenger ship sails past the Statue of Liberty and Ellis Island.

Today, Ellis Island's 27 1/2 acres is a national park containing the Ellis Island National Museum of Immigration.

America's vast natural resources needed workers to take the raw material and make it into usable goods. As cheap labor, immigrants took jobs in factories and mills, mines and farms. These jobs paid little, were physically difficult, and often dangerous. We don't know who Louis met when he got off the boat, but we do know that by September 1906 he had made his way to Colorado.

Though this view of Denver, Colorado was taken in 1898, Louis Tikas would have recognized it when he arrived in the summer of 1906.

Somewhere along the way, Louis learned enough English to become a kind of agent between his countrymen and the Americans. This skill made him a natural leader. Many young immigrants, up to fifty percent, only came to America long enough to make some money and go home. Louis planned to stay. In 1910, Louis went to the District Court in Denver to sign a paper called a Declaration of **Intention**. It was a first step in becoming an American citizen.

Living in Denver

Greek Town was the section of Denver where many Greek immigrants lived. Everyone there spoke the same language, shared a common background, and could share news from home. At first, Louis worked at a Greek coffee house in Denver. He probably met coal or gold or silver miners in the area. Later, he started work as a miner.

Miners and young mule driver in a Southern Colorado Coal Mine.
Oil lamps on hats suggest that the photo was take before 1900.

But Louis didn't stay just a miner. His ability to translate English for other Greek immigrants made him a valuable **commodity** to the United Mine Workers of America (UMWA). He could tell his fellow miners about the miners' union and how it could help them be safer on the job and get paid fairly. Company owners and operators were not happy to have people like Louis around. They preferred to have workers who came from many different nationalities and who spoke different languages. It meant they couldn't communicate in order to share complaints and organize. Men like Louis Tikas were a problem.

Louis became a UMWA organizer.

And a marked man.

Chapter 2:
King Coal

Trains moved coal across the continental United States.

Why was coal so important?

Coal is one of the three most important fossil fuels. Crude oil and natural gas are the other two. Coal has many uses, but in the early twentieth century, its importance was its value in the manufacture of steel.

Railroads provided a way to move goods vast distances. Oil needed to be moved from where the wells were to refineries and then on to those who needed to use it. By owning railroads businessmen could control the delivery of their own product.

Railroads require steel to build tracks and trains. Many early **industrialists** found it economical and **efficient** to own not only interest in, or outright ownership of, railroads but also the steel mills and coal mines needed to run them.

Without coal the steel mills could not turn raw ore into finished steel and many industries would falter. The hard **bituminous** coal found in mines like that in the Ludlow area was the best for making coke. Coking coal produces a high carbon fuel that burns especially hot. This coke is used in metal manufacturing processes. An extremely hot flame is necessary to melt and manipulate metal ores, particularly the iron ore used in steel manufacture.

Coal fueled the locomotives that made the railroad run. It also was sold to people and companies to heat homes and run steam powered engines in many industries across the country.

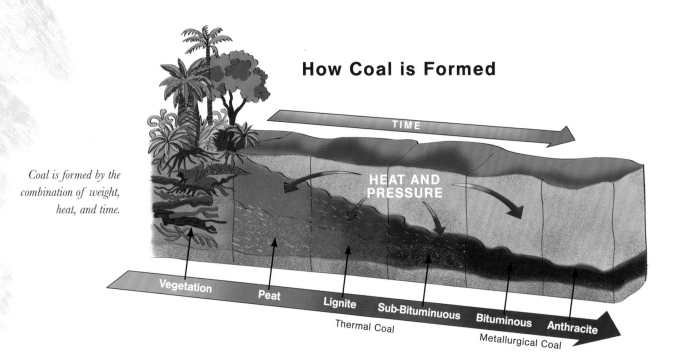

How Coal is Formed

TIME

HEAT AND PRESSURE

Coal is formed by the combination of weight, heat, and time.

Vegetation   Peat   Lignite   Sub-Bituminous   Bituminous   Anthracite

Thermal Coal

Metallurgical Coal

How Coal Forms

Coal, a **combustible** rock, began forming over 300 million years ago when southern Colorado was a vast swamp. It was created over **millennia** when plant matter died and accumulated under specific conditions. Often it piled up in swamp water which kept it from decaying.

A thick layer of plant **debris** is necessary to produce coal. The debris is covered by mud or sand. The weight of the mud or sand compacts the plant matter over time. This compaction over many hundreds and thousands of years creates coal. It takes about ten feet of thickness of plant debris to compact into one foot thickness of coal.

The geography of the Earth changes over time as the climate changes. Water flow changes the face of the planet. The forces within the planet's crust push some mountains up while creating desert where oceans once were. The Rocky Mountains were made in such a way. Hot **magma** from the earth's core pushed up over a long span of time until the swamps were gone and the coal that had been formed in them now became part of a mountain chain.

In some places, coal is found on the surface of the ground. But the most valuable **seams** lie below. When men discovered the usefulness of coal as a source of heat, they started digging. Coal mines were born.

BITUMINOUS coal is the most abundant. Fifty percent of the coal produced in the United States is bituminous.

PEAT is carbonized plant material. When buried and compacted for many years, it will become coal. Peat has been used as a heat source in many countries

ANTHRACITE is the highest rank of coal. It has the highest heating value per ton and is the coal most sought after for the manufacture of steel. It also is of great value to current day coal fired electric power plants because it burns cleaner than other ranks of coal.

LIGNITE is the lowest rank of coal. You can still see some plant debris in lignite.

Types of Coal

There are several different kinds, or ranks, of coal. The ranks depend on their carbon contents and how much compaction, called **organic metamorphosis,** has happened. Bituminous and anthracite coal are the two most important.

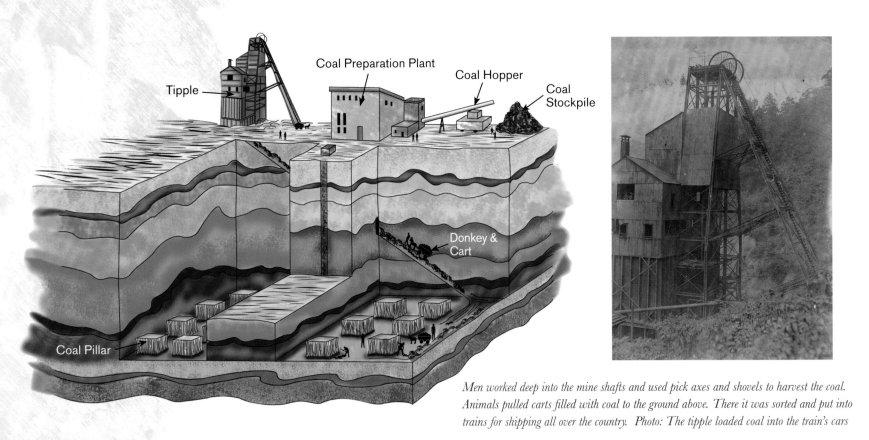

Tipple

Coal Preparation Plant

Coal Hopper

Coal Stockpile

Donkey & Cart

Coal Pillar

Men worked deep into the mine shafts and used pick axes and shovels to harvest the coal. Animals pulled carts filled with coal to the ground above. There it was sorted and put into trains for shipping all over the country. Photo: The tipple loaded coal into the train's cars

Coal Mining

At first Colorado coal was dug on the surface or from exposed seams on canyon walls. When the easy coal had been mined, mining companies started using explosives to get to deeper seams until finally, in the 1880's to 1890's they started going below ground.

Early miners learned to build ramps to reach the coal seams from above. They lay down rail lines and used animals to pull carts of coal from the working seam to the **tipple** above where the carts were unloaded onto railroad cars.

Most underground coal mining in Colorado was done by the "room and pillar" method. A very dangerous multi-step procedure was required. It meant drilling and undercutting into the coal bed and using dynamite to blast the coal. The coal was then loaded into carts and hauled up the mine shafts by mules, horses, or donkeys. Pillars of coal held up the ceilings of the rooms until the coal was played out. Then the miners would carefully excavate each pillar of coal, to get the most coal possible from each "room," as they moved on until the ceiling collapsed.

Chapter 3: The Dangers of Coal Mining

In the early 1900s, few roads were paved. Cars often broke down. The railroad, fueled by coal, provided dependable transportation for people and goods.

Why Choose Coal?

The American West held a **smorgasbord** of natural resources. Oil, coal, natural gas, gold, silver, and salt could all be found in abundance, if you had the resources to look for them and to **exploit** them. The vast area defied simple conquest. On the east coast, a network of rivers and waterways led the way to easy travel and movement of people and goods. But the west was desert and mountain. Rivers flooded one season and went dry the rest of the year. Even in high water years many western rivers were not navigable in any practical sense. By the early twentieth century automobiles were being seen in cities and, by the few who could afford them, in the sparsely populated rural areas. But the roads weren't very good and you had to have a sense of adventure to drive away from a populated area.

Railroads, and their ability to move large amounts of goods and people through all kinds of terrain and in all kinds of weather, became the transportation method of choice. Railroads needed coal. The coal from the southern coalfields of Colorado was perfect for the job.

Black Lung Disease

Black lung disease is caused by years of breathing coal dust. It usually is found in miners fifty years and older. It is called black lung because instead of healthy clean lung tissue, breathing even small amounts of coal dust over many years turns the tissue black as the coal dust builds up. It cannot be removed and causes thickening and scarring of lung tissue.

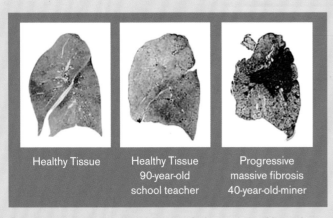

| Healthy Tissue | Healthy Tissue 90-year-old school teacher | Progressive massive fibrosis 40-year-old-miner |

Symptoms include coughing and shortness of breath that get worse over time. Sometimes the right side of the heart becomes enlarged which may cause heart failure. **Emphysema**, another disease of the lungs, is a complication. This disease cannot be cured, only prevented.

Lives Cut Short

Coal mining was hard and dangerous work. Miners spent up to twelve hours a day below ground. The only light came from headlamps. Dangers were everywhere. The wooden rafters that held up the roof of the tunnels could give way. The rock walls could collapse at any time, burying miners in tons of rock. Poisonous gas was always a possibility.

In the close confines of the mines, surrounded by seams of coal and wood holding the mine up, fire was a real danger. Coal dust is very combustible. Unseen gases seeping from the earth were, too. High explosives were used to blow hard rock walls and mishaps happened. Fires in the coal mines occurred easily if a spark from a miner's light ignited coal dust or gas.

Flooding was another threat since coal was created in swampy locations. Black lung, a disease caused by mining, could limit a miner's life significantly.

Loading coal into a cart.

Mules, horses, and even goats were used to pull the carts out of the mines.

Small birds, such as canaries, were brought into the mines to test the air quality. If the bird survived, the air was safe for the miners to breathe.

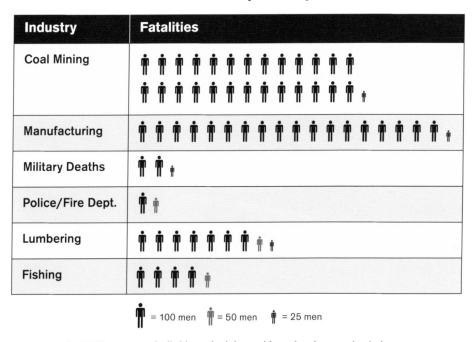

Annual Fatalities by Industry – 1913

Industry	Fatalities
Coal Mining	🧍🧍🧍🧍🧍🧍🧍🧍🧍🧍🧍🧍🧍 🧍🧍🧍🧍🧍🧍🧍🧍🧍🧍🧍🧍🧍
Manufacturing	🧍🧍🧍🧍🧍🧍🧍🧍🧍🧍🧍🧍🧍🧍🧍🧍🧍🧍🧍
Military Deaths	🧍🧍
Police/Fire Dept.	🧍
Lumbering	🧍🧍🧍🧍🧍🧍🧍
Fishing	🧍🧍🧍🧍

🧍 = 100 men   🧍 = 50 men   🧍 = 25 men

In 1913, more people died in coal mining accidents than in any other industry.

Being a coal miner in Colorado also made you twice as likely to be hurt or die from a mining accident than any place else in America.

In 1912 the fatality rate nationally in coal mines stood at 3.15 deaths per 1,000 workers. In Colorado the rate was 7.055 deaths per 1,000 miners.

Why was mining in Colorado so dangerous? The geology of where the coal was found was certainly a factor. Mine owners and operators were more interested in how much coal was brought to the surface than in the safety of the men who did the work. In some places, the donkeys that pulled the coal carts were considered of more value than the humans who filled the carts.

Miners were paid unfairly. By law, miners were supposed to be paid in currency, they were often paid in scrip. Scrip was basically an IOU from the mine owners to the miner that he had earned a certain amount of money. Scrip could only be spent in mine-operated company stores. Miners had little **recourse**. If they complained they could lose their jobs.

Samples of some types of scrip given to coal miners as wages. Scrip could only be used in the coal companies' own stores.

Miners were paid by the amount of coal they produced. Each miner's cart was weighed before being emptied into the tipple. The weigh man kept track of how much coal each miner produced. In many mines the weigh man was a company man who didn't mind reporting a much smaller number for a miner's work. This practice made more money for the company but the miner, who put his life in danger to dig out the coal, got short-changed.

According to a 1914 report by the congressional Committee on Mines and Mining, Colorado had good mining laws. Then why were there so many dangers? Perhaps the reason lurked in how the mines were managed. Only three inspectors worked for the state. They could not do the thorough job they needed to do in order to force **compliance**.

To mine owners, safety regulations were considered time–wasting government interference. Coal mine owners and operators often had local governments in their back pockets. Owners paid local officials bribes to ignore any rule breaking. This fact meant the owners controlled whether safety regulations were followed. The need for oversight in safety matters, as well as unfairness in how miners were paid, directly influenced the miners' desires to organize. They counted on men like Louis Tikas to help lead them to change.

Sixteen Tons tells the story of a coal miner who owes so much money to the company store that he can't afford to die. Authorship is generally given to Merle Travis though George S. Davis also claims to have written it.

Sixteen Tons was made famous by country singer Tennessee Ernie Ford.

Sixteen Tons

. . .You load sixteen tons,
what do you get
Another day older and
deeper in debt
Saint Peter don't you
call me 'cause I can't go
I owe my soul to
the company store. . .

Listen to the song: https://www.youtube.com/watch?v=Joo90ZWrUkU

Colorado Fuel and Iron Co., sample company housing in Primero, CO

Mining Camp Life

The camps and villages that grew up around coal mines were dismal places. Shacks made of wood or stone, drafty and small, would hold several miners or a miner's family. Rent for the housing was taken out of the miner's pay. He didn't have a choice of where to live since towns were often too far to walk on a daily basis and automobiles were rare and expensive. If the miners or family members were sick, they had no recourse but to use the company doctor. Food and other items had to be bought at the company store, at prices set by the company.

Something had to change. Miners and their families needed a way to make their lives better. Workers' Unions seemed to provide an answer.

Young boys and men too old or infirm to work in the mines worked as "breaker boys." Their job was to sort impurities from some of the smaller pieces of coal. They worked ten hours a day, six days a week.

The Work of a Marked Man

The coalfields of Colorado were divided into northern and southern fields. Louis Tikas began his work in the northern fields. By early 1913, union organizers (such as John Lawson, Ed Doyle, and John McLenna) began efforts to organize miners in the southern coalfields and prepared for a strike there. They hoped for a peaceful solution but prepared for possible violence. A UMWA office was set up in Trinidad, Colorado. Since many of the miners were Greek immigrants, Louis was sent south to lend a hand. His job was to exploit miner discontent and channel it into unionism.

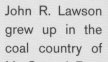

John R. Lawson (1871–1945)

John R. Lawson grew up in the coal country of Mt. Carmel, Pennsylvania. By age eight he was working as a **breaker boy** in a coal mine. Eventually he moved west. His first job in Colorado was at the Walsen Mine as a coal digger. He did not like the working conditions there or at any of the coal mines where he worked. The days were long and hard. He did not believe the pay was fair. But John was born and raised a coal miner. He became involved in work to organize coal miners into a union. He worked tirelessly all over Colorado standing up for coal miners' rights. He was involved in many strikes and became a major player in the 1913-1914 strike that led to the massacre at Ludlow. The last two years of his life were spent in the war manpower commission as a placement specialist during World War II. He died in Denver, Colorado on May 15, 1945.

Mine owners hired detective agencies like Pinkerton's or Baldwin-Felts to spy on miners who might be trying to organize a union.

Good Cop vs. Bad Cop: Union Organizers

Mine owners and supervisors saw union organizers as trouble makers who tried to make the miners realize how unhappy they were with the conditions in the mine. When the owners discovered an organizer, or agitator, they'd throw him out.

Union organizers worked for as little as $3.50 per day plus expenses. Many were beaten or killed. Sometimes they had to outrun detectives who worked for the mines' owners.

In 1913, the UMWA tried a different tactic. They started sending two-man teams to Colorado's southern coalfields. One man presented himself straight forwardly as an organizer, trying to get miners to join the union. The second man often was a man of the same ethnic origin as the miners. He became friends with the miners and built trust. He also built trust with the mine supervisors calling himself an anti-union man, saying he would turn in any miners who claimed to be union.

In fact, when the open organizer discovered a man who was against organizing, he'd pass the name to the inside man who in turn lied to the supervisor, telling him that the miner was pro-union, thus getting him fired. In this way by the time the union was ready to actively organize a mine, most of the anti-union miners had been fired by the mine supervisors through trickery.

Children as young as eight years of age worked in the coal mines.

Violence was a very real possibility. It had happened before. During a 1903 miner's strike in the northern coalfields, the strike was broken by beating miners, deporting immigrant miners, bringing in new immigrants to take the miners' jobs, and eventually calling in the Colorado National Guard to break the strike.

The 1903 Strike

The 1903–1904 coal strike in Colorado had many of the same elements as the strike that sparked the events at Ludlow in 1913–1914.

Miners in the Cripple Creek District decided to strike in 1903 to support union organization of the mills that processed the ore. The local government in Cripple Creek supported the unions. Mine owners in the Southern coalfields did not want their workers to unionize. They believed giving in to unions would dilute their earnings and their power.

Both sides used threats and violence to make their points. The mine owners also controlled the press. They made sure that they always looked good and the miners and unions looked bad. In this way they insured that the public never had the full story. They also had government officials and plenty of big money to back them up. By the time the strike ended in 1904 the Colorado Militia had taken over the town government and instituted **martial law**, much to the dismay of everyone else. In both the Northern and Southern fields, union workers were rounded up and marched out of the town, the county and the state.

So when similar events started happening in 1913, the mine owners already had a game plan they knew could work.

Chapter 4: Industrialists and Robber Barons

Cornelius Vanderbilt

John D. Rockefeller

Andrew Carnegie

Jay Gould

The Robber Barons

The original robber barons were **feudal** lords of the 12th and 13th centuries. Because these lords controlled access to bridges, waterways, and other places people needed to travel, they could demand money or goods to cross their property.

The term "robber barons" came into more modern usage after the Civil War. It described a handful of self-made men who built up great personal wealth by taking advantage of our country's rich natural resources. The growing immigrant population provided companies with a cheap but steady work force. The owners reinvested their wealth, took advantage of government programs and the lack of government supervision. They hired **lobbyists** to gain advantages with local and federal governments.

John D. Rockefeller Sr. (1839-1937) made his money by exploiting our country's growing need for oil. He established the Standard Oil Company and is widely accepted as the father of America's petroleum industry. His interest in railroads and coal were **offshoots** of this industry.

Other "robber barons" included Cornelius Vanderbilt (1794-1877), steamboats and railroads; Andrew Carnegie (1835-1919), steel; and Jay Gould (1836-1892), railroad financier. And while these men and their **ilk** certainly lived wealthy lives, perhaps by taking unethical opportunities and exploiting the poor and working classes, they also used their vast wealth to create and support **philanthropic** organizations, museums, and establish school and libraries.

Railroads carried coal. Coal was burned to turn iron into steel. Steel was used to build railroads.

The Rockefellers

Many mines in Southern Colorado were owned by Colorado Fuel and Iron, known as CF&I. CF&I's coal went to support its steel mill which supported the railroads. Coal was necessary to the production of the steel. It was cheap fuel for heating homes and businesses. Steel was necessary to make the railroads run. The Rockefellers, a New York family of wealthy industrialists, lived far away from the realities of Southern Colorado. They owned CF&I and its many **subsidiaries**.

John D. Rockefeller Jr. headed the company during 1913-1914. He had a man in Denver, Lamont Bowers, who oversaw the workings of the coalfield and sent regular reports to JDR, Jr.

Unfortunately, Bowers rarely visited the coalfields that he submitted reports on. In fact, he consistently told his boss in New York that everything was under control and that only a few trouble makers among the miners were interested in forming a union or were in any way unhappy with their lot.

John Davison Rockefeller Jr.

John D. Rockefeller Jr. was the only son of John D. Rockefeller, Sr., the founder of Standard Oil. He was educated at home until he reached ten years of age. His parents were very strict and **frugal**. He learned duty and responsibility early. When the family moved to New York in 1884, John Jr. began regular school. He was bright but had a nervous disposition that made him easily stressed. In 1893, John Jr., entered Brown University. His experiences in college brought him into contact with people and ideas that were new to him. He found the openness refreshing. John Jr. met his future wife, Abigail Aldrich, while at Brown. They married in 1901. After graduating from Brown in 1897, John Jr. went to work for his father at Standard Oil. John Jr. wasn't the rough-and-tumble business man his father was. Even so, John Jr. was given the responsibility of overseeing management of Colorado Fuel and Iron Company (CF&I).

John D. Rockefeller called his mansion in Sleepy Hollow, New York "Kykuit." This Dutch word means "lookout."

John D. Rockefeller Jr. lived thousands of miles from the coal mines he owned. This fact certainly had an impact on what he understood about the reforms union strikers were demanding. Rockefeller relied on business managers to provide him with reliable information. They did not always furnish it. And, the stark differences in how Rockefeller lived his life, as did the **progeny** of most of the Robber Barons, also played a role.

Mansions in New York and Chicago, huge estates with the unrealistic title of "cottage" on Long Island, New York and Newport, Rhode Island housed the wealthy. Servants catered to their every need. Their children were cared for by nannies and educated by tutors and in the finest schools. Rockefeller's home was a mansion in New York City. His family built another home in Sleepy Hollow, New York.

Workers' families who did not live in company housing might live in over-crowded tenements.

In contrast, those who worked in the mines and factories owned by the Robber Barons lived in company towns or in tenements in the cities. Tenements were large multi-family dwellings. They often had no heat or running water. In the mining camps many families were required to live in camp housing. Part of their pay went towards the rent. They bought food and supplies at the company store and could be turned out of their home and the town for any **infraction** of the rules.

Many mining towns had schools for the children. But with every dollar needed for survival boys as young as eight-years-old often quit school to work in the mines. Boys and girls alike worked long days in factories in the cities. Child labor laws were not enforced.

The children of the Robber Barons grew into the budding **philanthropists** of The Progressive Era. In the case of John D. Rockefeller Jr., the coal strikes in Colorado and the events at Ludlow in 1914 compelled him to change.

Thomas Woodrow Wilson
(1856–1924)

Thomas Woodrow Wilson was the twenty-eighth President of the United States. He was born on December 28, 1856, in Staunton, Virginia. His father, a Presbyterian minister, had a heavy influence in shaping Woodrow Wilson's strict moral code.

During his college years, Wilson decided to become a **statesman**. He achieved the **pinnacle** of this goal when he was sworn into office as the President of the United States in January 1913.

Wilson was not a fan of organized labor, but he needed their support to achieve his political goals. When their support helped him win his election to president, he offered labor leaders some influence in his administration. Ex-United Mine Workers official, William B. Wilson (not related to the president), was appointed head of the Department of Labor. Woodrow Wilson supported the Clayton Act which legalized unions and gave them the right to strike. His support afforded him strong allies in the unions.

Chapter 5: The Players - Conflict and Confrontation

President Woodrow Wilson

Two Sides

Deteriorating conditions for miners in 1913-1914 in southern Colorado made the possibility of a strike very real. The two sides were the United Mine Workers of America (UMWA), supporting the striking miners, versus the coal mine owners and operators. The participants ranged from **illiterate** immigrant miners all the way up to the President of the United States, Mr. Woodrow Wilson. The president didn't take sides, he just wanted the violence and the strike to be over so coal would move again.

With thousands of miners trying to organize you'd think the UMWA would have enough members to accomplish its goals. But it wasn't quite that simple. Money and politics controlled the opposing side. Besides the wealthy mine owners, Colorado Governor Elias Ammons—who managed the Colorado National Guard—became involved. These **factions** were supposed to be unbiased but were not. The sheriffs of Huerfano and Las Animas counties in Colorado also were included in this group. They did not like either the unions or the immigrant miners.

Who were all of these people and what made them tick?

United Mine Workers of America (UMWA)

The United Mine Workers of America was founded in 1890 in Columbus, Ohio. The UMWA wanted to limit miners to an eight-hour work day and fair pay. They wanted the right to **collective bargaining**. The union believed workers should be able to discuss whether labor laws were fair and safe. In 1913 these goals created a battlefield between workers and company owners. The UMWA strove to organize the miners into one voice to speak for all.

The early years of the labor movement were often violent and tragic. The UMWA wanted miners to be compensated for the wealth they created for the mine owners. Peaceful **arbitration** and settlement were the goals, but strikes often became necessary to force the owners' hands. In many cases, strikers were met with armed violence.

Coal miners armed themselves and prepared to strike.

Mary Harris Jones
(c.1830 – 1930)

Mary Harris Jones, also known as Mother Jones, immigrated to America from Ireland with her family when she was a child. The family moved to Canada where Mary grew up and attended a teacher's college. She worked in Michigan, Chicago, and Memphis, Tennessee, where she met her husband, George Jones, an iron molder. He was active in his trade union and Mary became interested, too. They had several children together. Sadly, George and the children died in 1867 during a yellow-fever **epidemic**. Mary moved back to Chicago where she opened a dressmaking business. Again misfortune struck. Mary's business and all her possessions burned in Chicago's great fire of 1871.

Mary began a new life stirring up workers to demand improved labor conditions. She had a talent for public speaking that moved and

continues on page 29

"Mother" Mary Harris Jones, (right), became active in the miners' quest for better pay and working conditions. She spent time helping the miners' families and working for a union.

Names and Faces of the Union

The UMWA had union organizers working for them. Louis Tikas was one of them as were John Lawson and Mary Harris "Mother" Jones. These organizers not only encouraged miners to join the union but rallied them and, once a strike was called, armed them. They took the brunt of **harassment** by those opposed to organizing a union and often were jailed.

Mother Jones traveled to Trinidad in southern Colorado, close to the mines, over and over. The sheriff arrested her and had her transported out of the county as soon as she was spotted. Mother Jones always returned. She hated bullies. She had a well deserved reputation as a rabble-rousing speaker and encouraged the miners to stand up for themselves against unfair labor practices.

Sheriff Jefferson Farr called himself the "King of the County."

The King of the County

Jefferson B. Farr, a large, red-haired man who was sheriff of Huerfano County, Colorado personified the **corruption** of county officials and coal mine operators. Farr was a Texan by birth but made his way to southern Colorado in the 1890's. He and his family bought land, cattle, and businesses, including saloons and the *Walsenburg World* newspaper.

continued from page 28

energized her audience. She appeared wherever labor problems occurred. In 1903 she went to Colorado under the support of the United Mine Workers. While there she worked undercover to find information that lead to the coal miners' strike in the northern coal fields. In late 1913 she went to southern Colorado to support the coal miners on strike there. She organized a women's march and was expelled from southern Colorado several times before she was imprisoned there for agitating the miners. Mother Jones spoke for working men and women and urged them to fight for their rights. Mary Harris Jones died in 1930. She was buried in Mount Olive, Illinois, at the Union Miners' Cemetery.

Elias Ammons
Governor of Colorado 1913-1915

Elias M. Ammons was born on a farm near Franklin, North Carolina, on July 28, 1860. Eleven years later his family moved to Colorado. During his life Ammons worked hauling lumber and railroad ties, was a nighttime street lighter, a journalist, a cattleman, and a banker.

Ammons' political life started in 1890 when he was elected to the State Legislature as a Republican. As a result of disagreeing with the Republican Party over adoption of the **gold standard**, Ammons switched to the Democratic Party. He was elected governor of Colorado in 1912 and served one term, from 1913 – 1915.

The coal miners' strike dominated his administration.

The Republican Party won the next gubernatorial election, in part because of the events at Ludlow. Elias Ammons later became president of Farmers Life Insurance Company. He died on May 20, 1925 and is buried in Denver's Fairmont Cemetery.

Sheriff Jefferson Farr hated the union organizers and found ways to intimidate them.

Jeff Farr was no friend to unions or union activities. Once he became sheriff he used his position to **disrupt** the miners' organization in many ways. He hired spies to eavesdrop on mine workers in his saloons. He paid miners to inform on other miners who were active in unions. He also deputized mine guards so that their violent treatment of the miners was covered by law – his law. He even chose jury members and told them how to vote. Many mine owners and operators slipped Jeff Farr money in order to have his support, in this way they escaped **liability** for mine accidents.

When one organizer was brought before Sheriff Farr to discuss his union organizing efforts, Farr told him, "I am the king of this county." Surprisingly, the people never revolted against Farr's form of law and order.

14—Colorado Fuel and Iron Company, Minnequa Steel Works, Pueblo, Colo.

Pueblo, a Thriving City with a Lasting Prosperity

2B-H421

A postcard photo of the Colorado Fuel and Iron Company. At one time, the company was the largest landowner and employer in the state of Colorado.

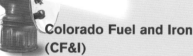

Colorado Fuel and Iron (CF&I)

Colorado Fuel and Iron (CF&I) was formed in 1892 when William Jackson Palmer's Colorado Coal and Iron Company merged with John C. Osgood's Colorado Fuel Company. CF&I operated both steel mills and coal mines in Colorado. It also held interest in iron mines, limestone quarries, and other materials involved in the manufacture of steel. At one time CF&I and all its holdings were owned by the Rockefeller family.

In its **heyday**, CF&I was the largest private employer and landowner in Colorado. The company changed hands several times after the steel market crash in 1982. CF&I closed the last of its mines in the early 1980's. After the firm went bankrupt in 1993, Rocky Mountain Steel Mills bought the company.

The coal mine owners and operators, led by CF&I, wanted to keep their mines open and operating at the lowest cost to themselves for the highest profit. Their aim was to keep the miners from organizing into a union. A union mine meant that collective bargaining would take place. Mine owners felt this change would put them at a disadvantage. They felt the miners should be grateful for their jobs and for the company towns where they lived. They felt collective bargaining for wages and conditions would decrease their profit and limit their control over how they operated their own mines. Mine operators preferred open shops where anyone could work, not a closed shop that was strictly union workers.

Chapter 6: Turmoil Begins

Lamont Bowers

Lamont Bowers

Lamont Bowers was John D. Rockefeller's representative in Colorado. He had the authority to speak for CF & I and for Rockefeller himself. Bowers believed unions were bad for business. He felt it was his job to hold the line on the company's expenses. He was not afraid to make hard decisions. When miners began their strike, he forced the miner's families out of their company homes. Bowers thought his tough actions would make the strike a short one. But, Bowers did not understand the determination of the striking miners and their families. His failure to inform Rockefeller of the true difficulties in Colorado cost the owner. Rockefeller not only suffered financial loss but also, in some ways, a loss of his reputation.

The Result of Bad Information

One of the reasons that things got so out of hand in southern Colorado was that CF&I owner John D. Rockefeller Jr. lived in New York. His agent in Colorado, Lamont Bowers, neither visited the mine sites nor sent factual reports to his New York boss. Even as tensions esclated in the southern coalfields, Bowers reported the miners were happy and that the union agitators were making the problems. He didn't have a firm grasp on the details of the situation because he relied on reports from the field himself. This behavior had consequences not only as confrontations grew worse, but in the future as Rockefeller was held responsible for his inaction.

The Miners' Demands

1. Recognition of the union and its right to bargain collectively.

2. A 10% wage increase on tonnage rates.

3. Enforcement of the eight-hour work day that was already law.

4. Payment for "dead work". This work included laying track, putting up timbers, handling impurities-work that didn't produce coal but was necessary for the operation of a mine.

5. The right to elect their own check-weighman without company interference. Check weighmen weighed the ore at the tipple, a miner was paid by the ton. The weigh man worked for the company and would "short" a miner to save the company money.

6. The right to trade in any store, select their own living places and doctors.

7. Enforcement of state mining laws and abolition of company guard system.

Given the money and power behind them, it would seem that the mine owners and operators could dictate terms. But the owners needed coal to be produced and miners to do the work. They believed that making any deal with any union would make them appear weak and encourage other workers to make their own demands. The owners and operators refused to meet with the miners if union organizers were involved.

After months of meetings and confrontations the miners, led by the UMWA, made demands. In September 1913 they declared they would walk out, go on strike, on September 23 if these seven demands were not met.

Union organizers address a group of coal miners.

Not only were the mine owners concerned, but Governor Elias Ammons was very worried. He wanted peace in Colorado and he knew that, in earlier conflicts with miners, the governor had been called upon to send in the National Guard, or state militia, to both keep the peace and get the mines operational again. He urged the mine owners to meet with the miners and union representatives, but they refused.

President Woodrow Wilson sent a representative to speak with John D. Rockefeller Jr. in New York, urging him to find a way to stop the strike. Rockefeller refused. He insisted that he trusted his representatives in Colorado to do the right thing. None of the reports he'd seen indicated that the situation was almost out of control.

So on September 23, 1913, to the surprise and consternation of the mine company owners and local and national government officials, the UMWA called a general strike. Between 10,000 and 12,000 miners walked out of the mines and refused to work.

When the miners and their families were thrown out of their company housing, the union helped set up this tent colony.

In preparation for the strike, the UMWA had leased ranch lands east of the company towns and mines. They had purchased tents and erected tent cities. The camp just to the north of Ludlow station was the largest site and became the headquarters for the miners and the union.

The mine owners took swift action. During what turned out to be a brutal early snow storm, they turned miners and their families out of their company housing, often without the time or the means to collect and transport their furniture and other personal items. The miners called themselves lucky if they managed to find a cart or a wagon to move themselves and their belongings to the camps set up by the union. Others only had time to grab the barest essentials before being forced into the elements to walk the miles to the nearest tent colony.

No one wanted a strike. The miners wanted to work. For immigrants like Louis Tikas, it was the reason they came to America. At the same time, they wanted fair and safe working conditions. The coal mine owners only made money if the coal was mined. Striking workers dug no coal. Stubbornness on both sides resulted in the strike. The same stubbornness created conditions ripe for rising violence.

Chapter 7: Confrontation at Ludlow

Detectives from the Baldwin-Felts Agency.

Scabs and Private Eyes

The protests and violence escalated on both sides as the strike stretched through the winter of 1913 and into the New Year. The mine owners brought in **scabs** to work in place of the striking miners. The miners, in turn, tried to stop the scabs from working in the mines because they made the strike less effective. They used verbal harassment against these new workers and non-striking miners and their families. When threats didn't work they moved on to physical violence.

The mine owners **retaliated** by hiring more mine guards. Often these men were also sheriff's deputies. This step made the guards' actions seem legitimate. In addition they hired the Baldwin-Felts detective agency to intimidate striking miners. These detectives, who had a reputation as strike breakers in the coal mines of West Virginia and other mines on the East Coast, were seen as nothing better than hired thugs by the UMWA and the striking miners.

The Death Special.

Machine of Death

In October a new weapon in the mine owners' **arsenal** made its first appearance: an armored car which the striking miners quickly named the Death Special.

It was a car covered with three-quarter-inch steel to protect the riders from bullets. A machine gun was mounted where the back seat would have been. Its range was up to two miles and it could fire four hundred shots a minute. A large spotlight sat on top of the dash. The car was built for intimidation and killing. And on October 17, the Death Special saw action.

On that rainy day, striking miners began taking shots at the tipple at the Forbes mine. They found cover above the mine on a rocky hillside. Mine guards returned fire. As the gunshots continued, women and children from the tent colony at Forbes took cover in a stone house. The mine officials called for help. Mounted deputies were the first to arrive followed by the Death Special holding eight mine guards.

It's unclear how the events unfolded, several different versions were given. However a mine guard was critically wounded by shots fired from the hillside. The Death Special took position about a hundred yards from the tent colony and the machine gun rattled some six hundred bullets at the thin, cloth tents. After it was all over, one tent had 150 bullet holes. One miner was killed, another severely wounded. A fierce storm descended and the gunfire stopped as combatants sought shelter from the weather.

General John C. Chase hoped that just the presence of the militia and their better weapons would help to avoid a strike.

General John C. Chase

John C. Chase was an eye doctor from Denver and father of six. He had experience breaking strikes. In 1903 Chase was part of the militia who used intimidation and violence to break the miners' strike in Cripple Creek, Colorado. He used many of the same tactics during the 1913-1914 coal strike.

Union Leaders React

The machine gunning of the Forbes tent colony had union leaders requesting help from Washington. Governor Ammons was upset by the violence provoked by the Baldwin-Felts gunmen to draw the strikers into violence. Ammons had an incomplete picture of who was responsible for the violence, he called the strikers, "armed murderers shooting at innocent people on the road." He refused to offer John Lawson, the union representative, assistance. Instead, on October 28, Governor Ammons ordered the Colorado National Guard to the southern coalfields. He hoped their presence would bring peace and get the mines producing again. The Colorado National Guard, under the command of General John C. Chase,

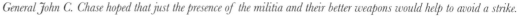

A Colorado National Guardsman aims a machine gun towards the striking miners.

entered the Ludlow area on November first. At first the miners greeted them with hope. The soldiers represented order and safety. The militia was to keep the peace only, not take sides. And for a while, that was the case. However before long mine guards were being accepted into the militia and the balance of power changed again.

The militia commanders ordered the miners to give up their arms to show their peaceful intent. The miners resisted but finally a few old rifles were surrendered. Eventually the militia organized peaceful and not so peaceful searches of striking miners' tents. No matter how many arms the militia seized, the striking miners always seemed to have more. In fact, the strike organizers made a point of buying rifles and ammunitions in Trinidad and Pueblo to insure that the miners could defend themselves.

General Chase had no love of unions or the striking miners. Against the wishes of the governor, he instituted **martial law**, where the legal rights and privileges of those he arrested were ignored. He became a law unto himself.

No Help from Washington

Through November and December of 1913 the situation became so dangerous that governor Ammons telegraphed President Wilson for help. Wilson, in turn, chided Bowers and Rockefeller to calm the situation. Bowers claimed that the situation was under control, as he believed what the mine operators told him. Rockefeller told the president he had complete faith in Bowers.

Even so, miners were injured and mine guards were killed in a continuing cycle of violence. Finally on November 26 and 27, Governor Ammons and Labor Secretary William B. Wilson met with representatives of the miners and the owners to try to reach an agreement. After fifteen hours of negotiating, everything but union recognition had been discussed. They decided to put the agreement to the vote of the miners. But without union recognition included, the miners overwhelmingly voted it down.

Mine owners pressured Ammons for more protection. To keep coal production up, Ammons finally directed the National Guard to protect new miners. The striking miners considered the new men strikebreakers and scabs and tried to intimidate them.

At the urging of Colorado congressman, Ed Keating, the U.S. House of Representatives subcommittee on mines and mining, headed by Congressman Martin D. Foster, began a series of hearings on the coal strike in southern Colorado in February 1914 in Denver, Colorado. It was called the Foster Committee. But events became more complicated. The state **auditor** of Colorado objected to the money being expended to pay for the militia in the southern coalfields. By the end of February, Governor Ammons withdrew all but 200 troops from the area because of limited funds.

In March, to counteract this reduction of professional soldiers, General Chase began accepting untrained mine guards, mine bosses, and **vigilantes** into the militia. These men, with

Congressman Martin D. Foster

no uniforms or training, were **designated** Troop A. By now the Foster Committee had finished its work in Colorado and moved on to Washington D.C. When John D. Rockefeller testified on April 6, 1914, he declared that he would neither change management of CF&I in Colorado nor bargain with any union.

The **impasse** continued.

Chapter 8: Tragedy

*Colorado National Guard
Lt. Karl Linderfelt*

Calm Before the Storm

On April 19, 1914, the Greeks among the striking miners at the Ludlow tent colony celebrated Orthodox Easter. In the pleasant spring weather they feasted, danced, and played baseball. It was more than a religious celebration, the whole tent community and even the militia and guards were invited and joined in the festivities. The day of peace resembled the calm before a storm.

John Lawson, the union organizer, wasn't in Ludlow on the morning of April 20. He left Louis Tikas in charge. Tikas had a way of smoothing out friction between the strikers and the militia. So when a woman complained to the National Guard that morning that her husband, a non-striking miner, was being held against his will at the Ludlow camp, Tikas was asked to answer the charge. He claimed the man was not in the Ludlow camp, but Major Patrick J. Hamrock, became nervous at the strikers milling about. He ordered the machine gun be installed on Water Tank Hill. Lt. Linderfelt took charge of the operation. Linderfelt saw the strikers as the enemy and the view from the hill would give the militia a military advantage. They'd be able to hit the tent camp with the machine gun fire from there.

Members of the Colorado National Guard Entering the Strike District

Even though Tikas told Hamrock that the man was not at the Ludlow camp, he was given a noon deadline to return him. Upon hearing this **ultimatum**, the striking miners began collecting their weapons, sure they would be attacked if the miner was not found.

Tension and suspicion ran high. Many women and children started making their way to the protection of the **arroyos** outside the camp. Other women and children began to take shelter in the dirt pits that had been dug under some of the tents as protection against gunfire.

Worried about the miners and their families in the camp, Louis Tikas urged them to stay calm while he went to speak with Hamrock at Ludlow station. When he arrived there, he saw the woman who claimed her husband was at the tent colony and was happy to tell her that the man had left the camp a day earlier. While Tikas was talking to Hamrock, Lt. Linderfelt and his men were riding up and down Water Tank Hill completing the machine gun placement. Their activity added to the general anxiety of the miners who saw a machine gun pointed at them as a threat. An attack seemed close at hand. Tikas wasn't there to calm them. Miners began to take their rifles and head for the hills outside the camp. Once the militia saw miners taking armed positions in the hills above, they became even more concerned.

From Militia to Mob

Tikas started back to camp waving a white handkerchief and hoping to calm the situation. Meanwhile miners began taking positions in the gullies along the train tracks and in pre-dug rifle pits and arroyos around the camp.

No one knew who fired the first shot. Each side pointed to the other. But bullets began to fly and people started to die. Tent walls were no protection against flying lead. The women and children left in camp sought protection underground. Others took shelter next to a train that stopped on the tracks until they could get away. Still more found a safe place in a pump house.

The battle raged for hours. The militia may have been outmanned, but they had superiority in fire power, and they used it. By now the camp was nearly unguarded as the miners fought from protected positions outside the colony. A group of militia, many from the untrained Troop A, swooped into camp intending to scare anyone left behind. A fire

The strike threatened the safety of the miners' families.

started. Later, observers stated it had been started by militia who were seen setting tents aflame. At the time no one knew that. In fact, it was discovered later that if cans of oil were found in the tents, the oil was poured on the canvas and set ablaze.

Tents were burning and militia men were looting. Pots and pans, clothing, jewelry, anything they could find, valuable or not, was stolen from the tents. The officers had lost control. The militia had become a mob.

Pits had been dug under some of the Ludlow tents. Women and children took refuge in the pits as the fighting continued.

Mary Petrucci had taken shelter with her three children in the pit below their tent. At one point she panicked and tried to run away from the pit and tent with the children. But the sight of the militia men, out of control, yelling and shooting, frightened her. She took her children to a pit under another tent, a larger space intended as a protected underground room for women about to give birth. The room was already occupied by Fedelina Costa and her two children, Patria Valdez and her four children, and Alcarita Pedregone along with her two children.

Crowded and afraid, the women and children waited as they heard the sounds of destruction above them. The crackle of flames from the tent burning above them added to their fear. They thought they'd be safe from the flames in the pit, but they didn't take the smoke into account. They could not escape. The fire stole the oxygen from the underground room. They all lost consciousness.

Louis Tikas and two other men were murdered by the militia.

A Leader is Murdered

Louis Tikas must have run from one catastrophe to another trying to help people and keep them safe. Eventually the militia officers tried to help the women and children escape the tent fires, but the miners' families didn't trust the militia. They had good reason to fear they would be killed and not taken to a safe place. Several tents exploded, probably from ammunition hidden inside.

As the soldiers took over the burning colony, Louis Tikas headed north, away from the camp. The militia headed in the same direction and eventually came across Tikas and two other strikers. Long simmering hatred against the man they called "Louis the Greek" boiled over. Lt. Linderfelt taunted Tikas, the two men argued. Linderfelt grabbed a rifle and broke it over Tikas' head. Louis fell but wasn't dead. Linderfelt left Sergeant Cullen in charge of Tikas and the other two prisoners. They wanted to hang the strikers. In the end, the militia shot Louis Tikas as he lay on the ground, unable to protect himself. They shot the other two men. Their bodies were left next to the railroad track for days because anyone who might have recovered them was afraid of being shot.

The Death Pit where two women and eleven children died.

Innocents Lost

Two women and eleven children died in what became known as the Death Pit. Amazingly, Mary Petrucci and Alcarita Pedregone survived. It was a long time before Mary, in particular, recovered emotionally.

Louis Tikas and five other miners died at Ludlow on April 20, 1914.

One National Guardsman died on that day as did one innocent bystander.

The results, especially the news of the women and children dying in the Death Pit, awoke the conscience of the country. It enflamed the anger and sense of helplessness of the striking miners. They took up arms and, for the next ten days, went to war against the unfairness and cruelty of mine owners and militia. They fought along the ridges, arroyos, and mines of the southern Colorado coalfields.

Four views of the Ludlow tent colony following its destruction.

Chapter 9: "Remember Ludlow!"

Miners and families returned to gather whatever belongings they could find.

The Need for Revenge

It wasn't until midmorning of April 21st that the bodies of the two women and eleven children were found in the Death Pit. Once the news reached Trinidad it was relayed to the outside world. The term "Ludlow Massacre" was **coined**. Enraged strikers swarmed into Trinidad. Outrage at the tragedy, against the militia's actions, and against the mine owners grew. The need for revenge grew within the ranks of striking miners who had fled Ludlow or those in the other mining camps who heard the news.

The National Guard tried to blame the fire on an accident, but witnesses came forward who claimed they saw the fire being spread by militia men with torches. Striking miners and their families in other tent colonies feared for their safety, thinking that if such horrific events could happen at Ludlow, they could happen anywhere.

General Chase was in Denver and Governor Ammons was in Washington D.C. when the tragedy occurred. Chase believed the burning of the Ludlow tent colony signaled an end to the violence. As soon as he heard of the deaths in Ludlow, Ammons cancelled the rest of his meetings and boarded a train for Colorado.

Strikers armed for war.

Avenging Ludlow

What neither General Chase nor Governor Ammons understood was the rage growing amid the ranks of the miners. John Lawson had set up a temporary headquarters in a place called the Black Hills in southern Colorado. Miners congregated there with guns and ammunition and considered what their next move might be. Lawson even told reporters, "It has now become a war of extermination." He also quoted John D. Rockefeller, Jr., who had once commented that he would risk his fortune against unions.

On Wednesday, a call to arms was issued by the unions to build an army. Outside donations poured in to help the strikers as well as funds from the UMWA **coffers**. Even before the call to arms, miners began attacking mines and mine guards. By nightfall, eight mines in southern Colorado were ablaze. The mines had been used as refuges for mine guards and their families. A state of civil war had descended on southern Colorado's coalfields. It would last for ten days.

You can see the small white coffins of the child victims as the horse-drawn cart carries them to the church.

Louis Tikas' funeral, April 27, 1914, Trinidad, CO.

Praying for the Dead

While the strikers waged their war, the bodies of those killed in and around Ludlow were prepared for burial. On Friday, April 24, a fragile truce was observed while the two women and eleven children who died in the Death Pit were buried in Trinidad. Fifteen hundred miners and their families lined the streets as the horse drawn carriages carried the coffins to the cemetery. Eleven small white coffins held the children.

The funeral for Louis Tikas was delayed as they waited for a priest from the Greek Orthodox Church to arrive to conduct the ceremonies. Tikas' funeral, along with that of two Greek compatriots, was held on Monday, following a funeral Mass.

The truce disintegrated shortly after the funerals and the violence picked up steam again.

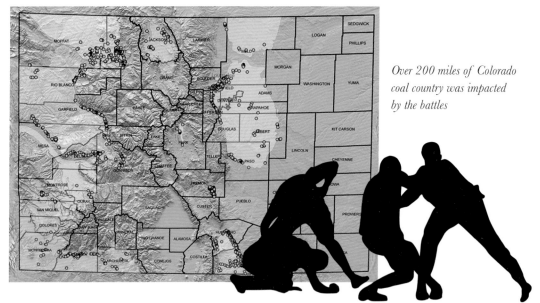

Over 200 miles of Colorado coal country was impacted by the battles

No Help from Leaders

Governor Ammons asked President Wilson for help. President Wilson's attention was turned to Mexico at the time. During the same week as the Ludlow Massacre the United States military was battling Mexican forces in Veracruz. Wilson didn't want to get involved in what he saw as Colorado's business. He asked Rockefeller to intercede, arguing that it was Rockefeller's mine and steel mills that would not make peace with the unions.

Rockefeller again declined to listen to any proposal that included recognizing a union. The **stalemate** continued even as Rockefeller commented to the White House that loss of property and lives would continue without federal intervention. He, as well as Governor Ammons,

wanted the president to send in federal soldiers to end the conflict.

While the politicians and industrialists talked, armed miners from outside of Colorado were joining the strikers in a steady stream. The war raged along the Front Range from Trinidad in the south to the coal mines of Louisville north of Denver—225 miles of conflict.

President Wilson finally authorized the use of federal troops on April 28, but not before a ten-hour gunfight broke out in Louisville and more people died. The miners seemingly attacked with a common goal, to destroy mine works regardless of the loss of life. Miners swept through the mine at Forbes and burned it to the ground. At least eleven men died.

Federal troops arrive.

APRIL

5	6	7	1 8	2 9	3 10	4 11
12	13	14	15	16	17	18
19	20	21	22	23	24	25
26	27	28	29	(30)		

Too Little, Too Late

A long, dragged out battle raged in Walsenburg, CO along the main thoroughfare between the mines and the middle of town. Private homes and business sustained damage and innocent bystanders worried for their lives. The militia was spread thin by this time and the strikers' ranks were growing. A cease-fire was called a week after the tragedy at Ludlow. The bodies of the dead combatants were collected.

Both sides, worn out from constant fighting, knew that federal troops were on the way. They agreed to continue the cease-fire until federal troops arrived.

On April 30, 1914, federal troops reached the southern Colorado strike zone. Their mission was to disperse all combatants, to keep the peace, and to relieve the Colorado National Guard. The militia was required to leave as soon as federal troops arrived.

The Colorado Coalfield War was over. In the ten days that it raged, fifty-four people, men, women, and children, died in the violence.

Chapter 10: Aftermath

Life after War

Mining restarted at CF&I owned mines and other mines, though without the striking miners. They still wanted union recognition and the UMWA supported them for a bit longer. In May 1914 the U.S. Commission on Industrial Relations began an investigation into the causes of the strike. They called John D. Rockefeller Jr. to speak. The Commission found that his long distance management and lack of action were largely to blame for both the strike and the increase in fighting that followed. Rockefeller seemed quite surprised by the strength of those speaking against him. He had trusted Bowers to tell him the truth about what was going on in Colorado since Bowers was so much closer to the action.

Some of the union women, including Mary Petrucci who survived the Death Pit, went on tour around the country to speak about what happened in Ludlow. They even went to Rockefeller's headquarters in New York City. While they sat in a reception room a sad looking man came out and looked at them, then went back into the office. He didn't say a word though they found out later it had been John Rockefeller Jr.

The Death Pit as it looks today at the Ludlow Memorial.

A Win or a Loss?

In September of 1914, President Wilson again presented a plan to end the strike in the coalfields. Again, the miners accepted the plan and the operators did not. In December of 1914, running out of money and wanting to shift their efforts and resources to other areas, the UMWA ended the strike. It appeared that the mine owners had won.

The UMWA purchased forty acres of the windswept and barren land in southern Colorado where the Ludlow camp had been in 1916. On May 30, 1918, they celebrated the opening of the monument they erected there to honor those who died on April 20, 1914. John D. Rockefeller Jr. attended, as did Mary Petrucci, who had lost her three children in the Death Pit.

The west side of the memorial. It says, "In memory of the men, women, and children who lost their lives in freedom's cause at Ludlow, Colorado. April 20, 1914. Erected by the United Mine Workers of America."

A statue, depicting a miner and a woman holding a child, was erected there along with a plaque with the names of all those men, women, and children, who died in Ludlow that day.

Unfortunately, 85 years later, on May 8, 2003, the statue was ruined by vandals. They cut off the heads of the man and the woman. They removed the woman's left arm. Even though a $10,000 reward was offered by the UMWA, the criminals were never found.

Miners around the world donated $80,000 to have the monument restored. The repaired monument was rededicated on June 5, 2005.

Compromise **TRUST**
SPIN safety well-being
health **no strike** court VOICE conviction
Company Union
guilty EXONERATED AFTERMATH
Fair trial **5-day work week** **listening**

A Kind of Compromise

The whole affair had Rockefeller going to visit his holdings in the southern Colorado coalfields as well as his steel mill in Pueblo in 1915. He spoke to the miners, the mine operators, and those who worked in the steel mills. What he learned compelled him to devise better ways of listening to and acting on worker concerns. While he remained against unions, he did institute company regulations that gave workers a voice in matters including safety, health, and pay. It was a "company union." The strike in the southern coalfields, and the way Rockefeller handled the aftermath, introduced a whole new way to "**spin**" public opinion. He became known as a philanthropist, a man who cared about the well-being of others, rather than a hard-hearted industrialist.

Some of the striking miners and mine organizers, such as John Lawson, were arrested for various acts of violence during the strike. Lawson was tried and found guilty of the murder of mine guard John Nimmo and sentenced to life in prison. However, the Colorado Supreme Court reversed his conviction two years later. The court found that the jury and the trial process itself had been influenced by the mine owners and their political representatives. Lawson had not been given a fair trial.

As for the National Guard officers and men, several were tried by a military court for their part in the strike and the massacre at Ludlow, but all were **exonerated**.

The Story of Mary Benich

Mary Benich McCleary 's parents, John and Dominika Benich, came from Yugoslavia. John was a coal miner. On April 20, 1914 the family was living in the Ludlow tent colony when the militia attacked. Mary was eighteen months old. John and Dominica grabbed Mary's two brothers and ran toward the railroad tracks. A train was stopped there. They hoped for protection from the flying bullets. In their panic they didn't realize Mary was missing until they reached the train. Several days passed before they were reunited with her. She had been rescued by a sixteen-year-old boy. Mary married during World War II. She and her husband raised four children. The family grew to include twelve grandchildren and thirteen great-grandchildren. Mary died in Morgan City, Louisiana.

Mary Benich McCleary

After the strike was over, many miners tried to go back to work in the southern Colorado mines. Many of the same mine guards who they'd fought against still worked at the mines. Many miners were "black balled," meaning their names were put on a list of men who were not welcome in the mines. But there were mines in other parts of the country who took the experienced miners. Or the miners found other work. Their experiences at Ludlow camp and the other mining camps stayed with them the rest of their lives.

The last known survivor of the Ludlow Massacre, Mary Benich McCleary, died of a stroke on June 28, 2007. She was 94 years old.

Folk singer Woody Guthrie memorialized the Ludlow Massacre in a song.

Ludlow Massacre
(Music and lyrics by Woody Guthrie)

It was early springtime when the strike was on,
They drove us miners out of doors,
Out from the houses that the Company owned,
We moved into tents up at old Ludlow.

I was worried bad about my children,
Soldiers guarding the railroad bridge
Every once in a while a bullet would fly,
Kick up gravel under my feet.

We were so afraid you would kill our children,
We dug us a cave that was seven foot deep,
Carried our young ones and a pregnant woman
Down inside that cave to sleep...

Listen to the song:
https://www.youtube.com/watch?v=XDd64suDz1A

Some Results of the Strike

Many striking miners, mine employees, family members, and innocent bystanders lost their lives in the Colorado Coalfield War. One historian lists seventy-five people among the dead. On the face of it, it would seem that the striking miners of 1913-1914 lost their battle for better and fairer wages, safety in the mines, and union recognition. However the events in southern Colorado, specifically in Ludlow, brought the attention of a nation to the plight of coal miners. Their sacrifices paved the way for the laws that regulate mining safety today.

The UMWA's goals may seem simple today, but only because of the battles fought and won by members in the early years of union organizing efforts. The eight hour work day, the right for collective bargaining, health benefits and health and safety protections all came about because individuals cared enough to fight for them.

Sheriff Jefferson B. Farr's "reign of terror" ended in 1916 when the Colorado Supreme Court declared the votes from the November 1914 elections from the coal precincts in Huerfano County invalid. Mine company interference with the elections was cited and Sheriff Farr was removed from office.

Farr was never prosecuted for his crimes. He died in March 1920.

Ghost Town: Ludlow, Colorado.

School yard, Ludlow, Colorado.

The Mining Town Today

Today what's left of Ludlow Station is a ghost town. It's ringed by barbed wire and privately owned. The falling down shacks stand mute testament to the violence that once erupted nearby. The train tracks still lie there, as do the tumbled stone works that once were part of a bustling mining community up the arroyos to the west. You can easily see Water Tank Hill and how a machine gun placed there would intimidate anyone within its range.

Men still work and die in coal mines. From West Virginia to Chile to China, men go down into the ground to dig out King Coal. The victims of the Ludlow Massacre, who were protesting for fairness and basic workers rights, will not be forgotten

Timeline

1879	William Palmer and four other men open the Colorado Coal & Iron Company.
1892	Palmer's Colorado and Iron merges with John Osgood's Colorado Fuel Company, forming Colorado Fuel & Iron Company (CF&I).
1903	Osgood loses controlling interest in CF&I to Rockefeller.
1903 – 1904	Miners strike across Colorado's coalfields.
1906	Louis Tikas immigrates to the U.S. He arrives in Colorado in September.
1910	Louis Tikas applies to become a United States citizen.
1912	Elias M. Ammons is elected governor of Colorado.
1912	United Mine Workers of America (UMWA) organizers intensify organization efforts in Colorado's southern coalfields.
1913, July	UMWA organizer, John Lawson, announces goal of unionizing all coal miners in Colorado, including the neglected southern coalfields.
August	UMWA, anticipating a strike, prepares by leasing land, tents, and other supplies outside the company towns/camps.
August 16	Baldwin-Felts agents (hired by coal companies) kill Gerald Lippiatti, a union organizer, in Trinidad, CO.
August 26	CF&I operators ignore two requests to meet with miners about their demands.
September	The coal miners draw up a list of seven demands and present them to the coal mine owners/operators.
September 23	The owner/operators ignore the demands and the southern coalfield miners, under leadership of UMWA, go on strike. Initially 9,000 striking miners and families are evicted from the coal company's company towns and housing. By the end of the month, 11,000 miners are on strike.

Timeline continued

1913, September 24   Bob Lee, a mine guard, is shot and killed by striking miners.

September 27   After 4 days without enough tents, and in bad weather, tents finally arrive at the tent colony set up by the UMWA near Ludlow. Thousands of miners and their families move into the Ludlow tent colony.

October 17   The armored car known at the "Death Special" makes its first appearance. One striker is killed when the car fires into the tent colony at Forbes.

October 24   CF&I guards shoot into a crowd in Walsenburg, CO, killing 3 striking miners.

October 25–26   Miners and guards skirmish in blizzard conditions. Guard, John Nimmo, is found shot to death. John Lawson will be tried for his murder.

October 26–28   Striking miners attack Berwind and Hastings coal camps.

October 28   Colorado governor, Elias M. Ammons, finally orders the Colorado National Guard to the southern coalfields in hopes of creating and keeping the peace and getting the mines producing again. General John C. Chase is the commanding officer.

October 30   President Woodrow Wilson steps into the fray asking CF&I officer why they keep rejecting UMWA counsels of peace.

November 1   The Colorado National Guard reaches the Ludlow area.

November 20   George Belcher, a Baldwin-Felts security guard, is shot to death in Trinidad, CO, by striking miner, Louis Zancanelli.

November 26   Colorado governor Ammons and U.S. labor secretary manage to get miners and coal operators to work out an agreement. It does not include union recognition and the miners vote to reject the agreement on November 30.

December 16   The State Federation of Labor meets in Denver. On the agenda: militia cruelty, intimidation, and arrests of miners without due process.

Timeline continued

December 17	Mother Jones leads a protest march to the capitol building in Denver.
1914, January 4	Mother Jones is arrested by the militia in Trinidad and put on a train back to Denver. She returns to Trinidad on January 11 where she is put under "house arrest" in San Rafael Hospital.
January 23	One thousand miners' wives march in solidarity for Mother Jones.
January 27	Congressman Edward Keating wins approval to investigate the Colorado coal miners strike.
February 9	Congressman Martin Foster chairs hearings in Denver by the U.S. House Subcommittee on Mines into the causes of the strike.
February 27	Because of large expense of keeping the militia in the southern coalfields, Governor Ammons begins withdrawal all but 200 from the strike zone.
March 10	The militia is ordered to tear town tents in Forbes tent colony because of a suspected criminal hiding there.
March 28	Most of the Colorado National Guard is removed from the strike zone. Two companies are left, most of them are mine guards, hired guns, and sheriffs deputies.
April 6	John D. Rockefeller Jr. tells the Foster Committee in Washington, DC that he supports the open shop principle. Anyone can work in an open shop, not just union members.
April 14	The militia's numbers are reduced further leaving mine guards, pit bosses, and vigilantes to fill in.
April 20	The Ludlow Massacre occurs when National Guard troops fire into the tent colony then set it on fire. Twenty strikers, including the 11 children and 2 women in the "death pit" die. Louis Tikas is killed.

Timeline continued

April 21–May 1	The ten-day Colorado Coalfield War occurs as strikers avenge the deaths at Ludlow.
April 25	Governor Ammons wires President Wilson asking for federal help.
April 27	Several thousand march at Louis Tikas' funeral.
April 28	President Woodrow Wilson orders federal troops into the strike zone to establish and keep the peace.
April 30	Federal troops arrive in the strike zone, Colorado National Guard troops are relieved.
May	The U.S. Commission on Industrial Relations investigates the causes of the strike. John D. Rockefeller Jr.'s management and lack of action are largely blamed.
September 5	President Wilson presents the Farley Davis truce plan to the miners and operators. The miners accept it but the operators do not.
December 7	Union leaders vote to end the strike, they have run out of money to continue.
1915, January	Federal troops leave Colorado's southern coalfields.
January 25	John D. Rockefeller Jr. again testifies before the U.S. Commission on Industrial Relations.
April 21	John Lawson is found guilty of the murder of mine guard John Nimmo and sentenced to life in prison. The conviction is reversed by the Colorado Supreme Court two years later.
September	John D. Rockefeller visits CF&I mines in Colorado. He talks to the miners and hears from them first hand, for the first time, instead of through intermediaries. He proposes an Industrial Representation Plan, essentially a company union to make sure worker grievances are heard. The miners vote to accept.
1916, June	Huerfano County Sheriff Jeff Farr is removed from office after the Colorado Supreme Court declares the election of 1914 invalid.

Glossary

anthracite coal (AN thruh site KOHL) A type of coal that looks shiny and doesn't give off much smoke when it is burned.

arbitration (AR bi TRAY shun) The process used to help two opposing sides reach an agreement.

arroyos (uh ROI uhss) A gully or channel that has been carved by water.

arsenal (AR suh nuhl) A collection of weapons or, a place to keep and store weapons.

auditor (AW di tur) A person who examines business accounts.

bituminous coal (buh TOO muh nuhss KOHL) A soft coal that contains a tar-like substance. It does not burn as cleanly as anthracite coal.

breaker boy (BRAYK ur BOI) A coal-mining worker whose job was to separate impurities from coal by hand. Boys too young to be in the mines and men to old or ill to work there often were used as breaker boys. Their work day was 14 to 16 hours long.

coined (KOIND) Invented a new word or phrase.

coffers (KAW furz) Boxes or places where money is kept.

collective bargaining (KUH lek tiv BAR guhn ing) Discussion about wages, work hours, and medical benefits between an employer and the members of a union.

combustible (kuhm BUSS tuh buhl) Able to catch fire; able to burn.

commodity (kuh MOD uh tee) A good that can be bought or sold.

compliance (kuhm PLYE uhnss) Obeying a command or suggestion.

corruption (kuh RUP shuhn) Making something bad or dishonest.

debris (duh BREE) The broken pieces of something that has been destroyed.

designated (DEZ ig nate uhd) Chosen; named.

dispersed (diss PURST) Scattered.

disrupt (diss RUHPT) To break up something that is going on.

efficient (uh FISH uhnt) Not wasting time or energy.

emphysema (EM fuh SEE muh) A lung disease often caused by smoking or by constantly breathing in tiny particles of dirt, coal, or wood.

epidemic (ep uh DEM ik) The quick spread of diseases in a population.

exonerated (eg ZON uh rate uhd) Freed from blame.

exploit (ek SPLOIT) To use or treat a person unfairly.

factions (FAK shuhnz) Small groups existing as part of a larger group.

feudal (FYOO duhl) A system established during Medieval times in Europe. A wealthy lord or land owner would give homes and protection to people who worked and fought for him.

frugal (FROO guhl) Careful not to waste money or things.

gold standard (GOHLD STAN durd) A system that says a certain type of paper money is equal to a certain amount of gold held by a government.

harassment (huh RASS muhnt) The act of pestering or annoying someone.

heyday (HAY day) The best time of a person's life.

ilk (ILK) Sort; kind; type.

illiterate (i LIT ur it) Not able to read or write.

impasse (IM pass) A situation or problem for which there is no solution.

industrialists (in DUHSS tree uh listss) People who own or run factories.

infectious diseases (in FEK shuhss duh ZEEZ uhz) Illnesses that can be spread from person to person.

infraction (in FRAK shuhn) A broken rule or law.

intention (in TEN shuhn) Something a person means to do.

liability (LYE uh BIL uh tee) A problem, debt, or disadvantage.

lignite (LIG nyte) Also called brown coal. Lignite is ranked between bituminous coal and peat. It contains some plant fibers and does not burn as well as other types of coal.

lobbyists (LOB ee istss) Groups of people who work to get politicians to pass certain laws or vote in a certain way.

magma (MAG muh) Melted rock that flows out of volcanoes or is found under the earth's surface. Cooled magma becomes igneous rock.

martial law (MAR shuhl LAW) Ruled by the army or military rather than by elected officials.

millennia (muh LEN ee uh) Several periods of one thousand years each.

offshoots (OFF shoots) Things that develop from other things.

organic metamorphosis (or GAN ik MET uh MOR FUH siss) The complete change that occurs in a living thing or a product of nature.

peat (PEET) Partly decayed plant matter usually found in bogs or swamps that can be dried and burned for heat.

philanthropic (fi lan THRAW pik) Giving charity to the needy.

philanthropists (fuh LAN thruh pistss) People who give time or money to help others.

pinnacle (PIN uh kuhl) The top of a mountain. Also, something that is the best example of a thing.

progeny (PRAW juh nee) Children.

recourse (ri KORSS) Help; aid; assistance.

retaliated (ree TAL ee ate uhd) Took revenge; fought back.

scabs (SKABZ) People who take jobs from striking union workers.

seams (SEEMZ) Bands of metals or minerals in the earth.

smorgasbord (SMOR guhss bohrd) This word originally meant a table set with many choices of food. It can also mean a great number of choices of things or actions.

spin (SPIN) To say things or relate a story in such a way as to sway how people think.

stalemate (STAYL mayt) A point in an argument or competition where neither side can win.

statesman (STAYTSS muhn) A great leader in government.

steerage (STIHR uhj) The section in a ship for people who payed the lowest fare to travel.

subsidiaries (suhb SID ee ER eez) Companies which are controlled by other, larger companies.

tipple (TIP puhl) A machine used to fill railroad cars with coal.

ultimatum (uhl tuh MAY tuhm) A final demand accompanied by a threat of punishment.

vigilantes (vij uh LANT eez) People who decide to take the law into their own hands.

Index

Photo credits

Page 6 Library of Congress

Page 7 Library of Congress

Page 8 Library of Congress

Page 9 Colorado History Museum

Page 11 Courtesy of USGS

Page 12 Library of Congress

Page 13 Library of Congress

Page 14 (left) National Institute of Safety and Health; (center) National Institute of Medicine; (right) Center for Disease Control

Page 15 Mining Safety and Health Administration

Page 16 (left) Library of Congress

Page 17 Library of Congress

Page 18 Denver Public Library

Page 19 Library of Congress

Page 21 Library of Congress

Page 23 (left) Colorado History Museum; (right) Library of Congress

Page 24 Kris/Flickr.com

Page 25 Library of Congress

Page 26 Library of Congress

Page 27 Denver Public Library

Page 28 *The Autobiography of Mother Jones by Mother Jones*, 1837-1930, Edited by Mary Field Parton, 1878-1969, Introduction by Clarence Darrow, 1857-1938. Chicago: Charles H. Kerr & Company, 1925.

Page 29 Mother Jones Library of Congress Jefferson Farr courtesy of the Huerfano County Historical Society – Francisco Fort Collection

Page 31 Courtesy of Colorado Fuel and Iron Company

Page 32 *Blood Passion: The Ludlow Massacre and Class War in the American West*, Scott Martelle. New Brunswick, NJ: Rutgers University Press, 2008.

Page 33 @2017 Jupiter Images.com

Page 34 Denver Public Library

Page Wikipedia

Page 36 Wikipedia

Page 37 Denver Public Library

Page 38 Denver Public Library

Page 39 Denver Public Library

Page 40 Denver Public Library

Page 41 Library of Congress

Page 42 Denver Public Library

Page 43 Denver Public Library

Page 47 Denver Public Library

Page 48 (top left) Library of Congress, (top right) Wikipedia, (bottom left) Wikipedia, (bottom right) Library of Congress

Page 49 Library of Congress

Page 50 Denver Public Library

Page 51 Denver Public Library

Page 53 Denver Public Library

Page 55 Courtesy of K. D. Huxman

Page 56 Courtesy of K.D. Huxman

Page 59 Library of Congress

Page 60 Courtesy of K.D. Huxman

Illustrations credits

Cover; title page; pages 5, 10, (left) 12, 16, 20, 22, 30, 33, 44, 45-46, (right) 52 , 54, 57-58
by Lisa Greenleaf

Special Thanks

Acknowledgement

I could not have done this without the information accessible from the Pikes Peak Library District, both the online databases and the Special Collections department. With thanks to every historian and researcher who came before me. ~K.D. Huxman

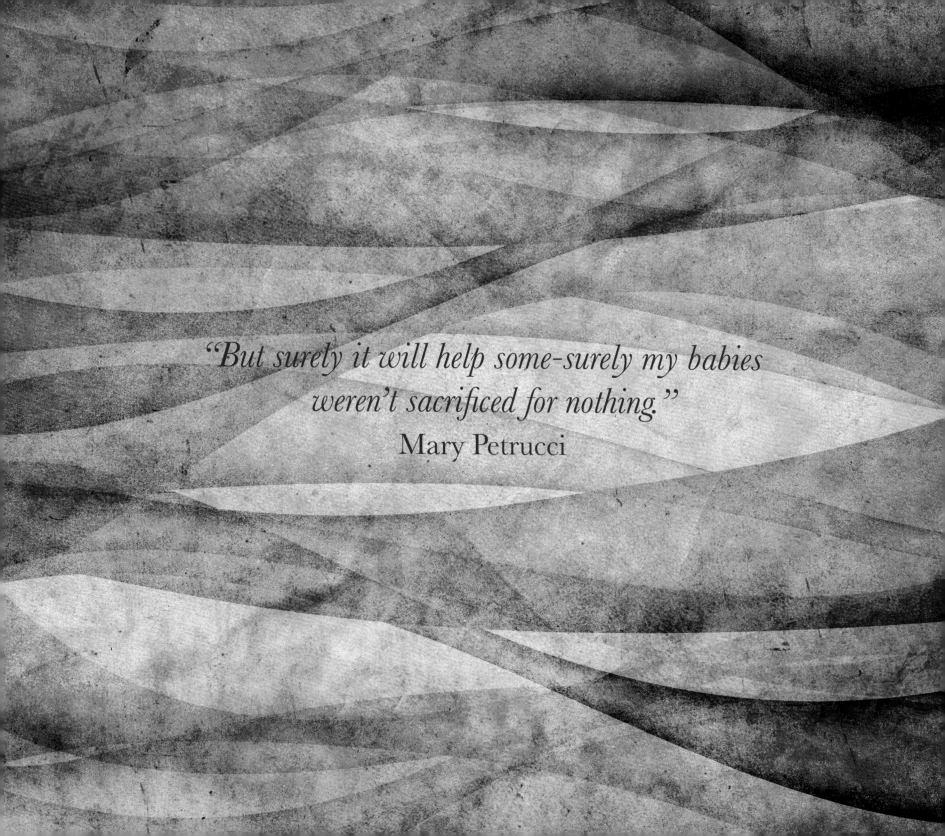

"But surely it will help some-surely my babies weren't sacrificed for nothing."
Mary Petrucci

Colorado Coal Field Summary

This is what life was like in a coal mining town in the early 1900s: children as young as eight years of age worked 12-hour days, six days a week. Men died in preventable accidents. If the work did not have to do with the actual harvesting of coal, the men were not paid. The pay they did receive was a type of fake money called scrip. It could only be used in stores owned by the coal company. Families were forced to live in shacks provided by the company. Many workers were immigrants, willing to take any job in order to make a living in their adopted country.

When coal miners decided they wanted a fair and safe working environment, mine owners refused. The only thing that might create a change was a fight. The fight went beyond arguments and skirmishes.

The fight became war.

About the Author

Karin (K.D.) Huxman is the author of nine adult romance novels, two children's picture books, and is a contributor to Apprenticeshop Books *America's Notable Women Series*. She is also a published poet and short story and magazine author. Karin attended the University of Lowell where she obtained a B.S. in Biology. She served five years in the Air Force, moving through the officer ranks to captain. She ultimately earned an M.F.A. in Writing for Children and Young Adults from Vermont College of Norwich University in 2001. Her picture book, *Grizzelda Gorilla*, won the Eppie Award in 2008 for Best Children's/Young Adult ebook. When she's not at work at the local library, you can find her walking, working on her yoga poses, or trying to coax anything to grow in the arid climate of the Pikes Peak region in Colorado. www.kdhuxman.wordpress.com or email her at k.d.huxman@att.net

About the Illustrator

Lisa Greenleaf is an award-winning illustrator and author. Her images and stories have graced many children's books including, *John Greenleaf Whittier's The Barefoot Boy*, *Feathers & Trumpets A Story of Hildegard of Bingen*, *When Rivers Burned: The Earth Day Story* and the *America's Notable Women Series*.

Lisa continues to follow her passion for art and design and has a successful design business, *Greenleaf Design Studio*. She has been featured in the news, TV, radio, art shows and book events. Lisa is an accomplished motivational speaker and has made many presentations at events and programs, sharing her stories, anecdotes, inspirational messages, music and tools that she incorporates throughout her work and daily life. www.Lisagreenleaf.com, Lisa@Lisagreenleaf.com